ABIDING IN
Christ

30 DEVOTIONS
FOR WOMEN

ABIDING IN

Christ

30 DEVOTIONS
FOR WOMEN

FAITH MILLER
WITH VINCE MILLER

EQUIP PRESS

Colorado Springs

ABIDING IN

Christ

Published by Equip Press, Colorado Springs, CO

First Edition: 2019
Abiding in Christ / Faith Miller
Paperback ISBN: 978-1-946453-93-8
eBook ISBN: 978-1-946453-94-5

EQUIP PRESS

Colorado Springs

TO: _____

FROM: _____

NOTE: _____

_____

_____

_____

_____

_____

_____

_____

_____

_____

_____

_____

_____

_____

_____

_____

_____

A NOTE FROM THE AUTHOR

I feel blessed to have the opportunity to share the stories of great faith that follow. I pray that through each of these devotionals, you are motivated by God's Word to live a life of unconditional faith in Christ. It can be so easy in this day to fall into a pattern and so difficult to trust what we can't see. My hope is through this devotional, you are able to do three things. First, be welcoming to God's Word. Let the verses speak to you and be willing to dig deeper into what God is saying to you personally. Second, let the words guide you to a discussion with another woman. As women, we strive to be strong but too often shy away from conversations of our faith due to fear of rejection. Go beyond the surface level conversations and dive into God's Word with another woman. Third, be open to the virtues laid out before you. Let each devotion shape you in your journey of faith.

— *Faith Miller*

ABOUT FAITH MILLER

Faith Miller grew up in a Christian home and considered herself blessed with the love and support those around her provided. From a young age, she watched as her father, Vince Miller, shared the stories of struggles from his childhood and the man who brought him to faith, his grandfather. She saw the impact his stories made on those around him and the number of people who were motivated by his desire to provide mentorship.

When her father founded Resolute, he inspired men to live with greater conviction, become mentors, and be mentored. She watched as thousands of men were inspired to overcome hurdles presented by living as a man of faith. She also noticed the number of women who came to him in hopes of finding the resources they craved. Women seemed to constantly be asking if he had something for them, as they had been living with many of the same problems. Therefore, Faith realized how much of a struggle it was for not only men but women as well.

Faith is currently living in St. Paul, Minnesota and is completing her degree at Bethel University. She is an enthusiastic leader who has a commitment to communicating God's Word. Faith is following in her father's steps to create resources for women that inspire them as much as he has inspired men.

USING THIS BOOK

THE PURPOSE

This 30-lesson devotional is for women to use in private reflection or conversations with other women. It is written to invite character development conversations for women of any age, as well as spiritual development, and can be used repeatedly.

THE PROCESS

ONE | ABIDE

Read through one virtue each week and answer the questions within the lesson. Each lesson uses our A.B.I.D.E. process.

- ADMIT the feeling the topic incites.
- BRING thoughts and issues to mind.
- INFORM new thoughts from the Bible.
- DETERMINE action steps.
- EXECUTE one action for one week.

TWO | PARTNER UP

Take each lesson further by partnering up with another woman. Use the 30 lessons as a mentoring and discipleship tool that takes all the guesswork out of a spiritual conversation. Partner up with a friend, neighbor, church member, associate, or relative.

THE PAYOFF

If you stay with the process for all 30 lessons, you will grow in character as a woman of God. Often, women just need a plan to get moving spiritually. This book is a plan - a method and a process that results in outcomes with a rich spiritual payoff.

CONTENTS

LOVING

In this is love, not that we have loved God but that he loved us and sent his Son to be the propitiation for our sins. Beloved, if God so loved us, we also ought to love one another. No one has ever seen God; if we love one another, God abides in us and his love is perfected in us.

– 1 JOHN 4:10-12

The word *"love"* is thrown around more and understood less than almost any other word in our vocabulary. It is a robust, relational word, and people across the world express it in many unique ways. Love's compassion fuels songs, poetry, and art. We use the word love to describe our hair, our clothing, and the food we savor. The bond between a husband and wife, a parent and child, or two friends are all considered a display of love. This one word is used in so many ways that there is plenty of confusion around what it means to love.

According to the Bible, God is not just a loving God - he is actual Love. It is one of the few things Scripture says is fundamental to his being. God is, therefore, the baseline for unpacking this critical and incredible word. And God's model of love is the life of Jesus. His actions, character, and integrity are the standard for love. So if you want to understand love, you have to know Jesus and the life he led. The very life he laid down as a loving friend so that you might know the love of God.

Prayer

GOD, too often I won't let you love me. I often feel unworthy, broken, and far from you. But today, I am asking and inviting you to love me. I no longer want to remain at arm's length from you and your endless love. Demonstrate your love for me, your child.

REFLECTION & DISCUSSION

ADMIT: What feelings does this topic invoke?

BRING: What issues do you need to address?

INFORM: What does the text say to do?

DETERMINE: What steps do you need to take?

EXECUTE: What action will you take?

FLOURISHING

I am the true vine, and my Father is the gardener. He cuts off every branch in me that bears no fruit, while every branch that does bear fruit he prunes so that it will be even more fruitful. I am the vine; you are the branches. If you remain in me and I in you, you will bear much fruit; apart from me you can do nothing. If you do not remain in me, you are like a branch that is thrown away and withers; such branches are picked up, thrown into the fire and burned. If you remain in me and my words remain in you, ask whatever you wish, and it will be done for you. This is to my Father's glory, that you bear much fruit, showing yourselves to be my disciples.

– JOHN 15:1-2, 5-7

*G*ardening is a process that demands time and attention before you can achieve the desired result. If you plant seeds and then abandon the garden until harvest, you won't find much produce in the middle of all the weeds. In this parable, God is the gardener. We learn that productivity is important to God, and so he does what is necessary in his people to cause the desired result. He removes the unproductive branch and even prunes the productive one. As a branch, you have one job, and it is not what you may think!

The responsibility of a God-fearing woman is to *"remain"* in the vine. The most productive activity is to stay connected to the source of nutrients. Stay connected, and the outcome will always be fantastic. Recognize it's God who prunes and tends to the branch, while Jesus is the lifeline. Become familiar with your role so that you don't try to overcompensate by getting in God's way. Accept the wounds that come with pruning, fully trusting the Gardener. Let time with Jesus nourish you. Give evidence to your discipleship by remaining in Christ and leaving the results up to him.

Prayer

GOD, my role is surprising here. I can see that sometimes I get in your way. Give me strength and help me understand what it means to remain in you. And, God, boldly I pray you will prune me so that I will flourish.

REFLECTION & DISCUSSION

ADMIT: What feelings does this topic invoke?

BRING: What issues do you need to address?

INFORM: What does the text say to do?

DETERMINE: What steps do you need to take?

EXECUTE: What action will you take?

PERSISTING

And he told them a parable to the effect that they ought always to pray and not lose heart. He said, "In a certain city there was a judge who neither feared God nor respected man. And there was a widow in that city who kept coming to him and saying, 'Give me justice against my adversary.' For a while he refused, but afterward he said to himself, 'Though I neither fear God nor respect man, yet because this widow keeps bothering me, I will give her justice, so that she will not beat me down by her continual coming.'"

– LUKE 18:1-5

*A*s a mother, who can ignore the child that persistently pesters? Anyone who has children or has been around children knows how they can insist on the things they want. When you are under bombardment, it is hard to do anything but say yes. And in this text, Jesus connects this determined behavior to the practice of prayer.

Your relationship with God is meant to be uninterrupted and perpetual. As such, you should assume that God is invested in everything you feel and experience. He wants you to come to him all the time – as any good parent would. Jesus demonstrated this practice of open communication with God in his own prayer life. And in 1 Thessalonians 5:17, the apostle Paul teaches that you should *"pray continually."* So as a good daughter, persist in prayer.

Prayer

GOD, I commit this day to persistent prayer. While I often come in seasons, or only in moments of need, today will be a day of ongoing communication with you. Know my desires and hear my prayers today.

REFLECTION & DISCUSSION

ADMIT: What feelings does this topic invoke?

BRING: What issues do you need to address?

INFORM: What does the text say to do?

DETERMINE: What steps do you need to take?

EXECUTE: What action will you take?

IMMERSING

Do you not know that all of us who have been baptized into Christ
Jesus were baptized into his death? We were buried therefore with him
by baptism into death, in order that, just as Christ was raised from the
dead by the glory of the Father, we too might walk in newness of life.
– ROMANS 6:3-4

*S*ometimes you need to restart. We have all had projects where a complete rebuild was required, where a simple remodel and readjustment were not enough. No, it was necessary to tear apart everything so that something new could be built. For Christians, baptism is a symbol of this type of restart. It's the point at which our new life begins.

Jesus led the way in showing all people how to launch into a new life through the waters of baptism - even though he was without sin, he modeled for you this act of repentance and rebirth. Baptism or *"immersion"* into the death of Christ is the way you restart your new life. You must do this because you cannot improve your life as it exists today; you must die to the life you have lived and begin a new life in Christ. It is a complete burial of the old and a resurrection into a new life. And the act of baptism is a representative symbol for all believers.

Only God, through Jesus' death and resurrection, could create the new life you so desperately need. David longed for this redemption in Psalm 51:10, praying, *"Create in me a clean heart, O God; and renew a right spirit within me."* The good news is that you have this opportunity through Jesus Christ.

Prayer

GOD, I choose today to bury my old life with its wants and desires, and today I begin a life made new.

REFLECTION & DISCUSSION

ADMIT: What feelings does this topic invoke?

BRING: What issues do you need to address?

INFORM: What does the text say to do?

DETERMINE: What steps do you need to take?

EXECUTE: What action will you take?

SUBMITTING

But the centurion replied, "Lord, I am not worthy to have you come under my roof, but only say the word, and my servant will be healed. For I too am a man under authority, with soldiers under me. And I say to one, 'Go,' and he goes, and to another, 'Come,' and he comes, and to my servant, 'Do this,' and he does it.' When Jesus heard this, he marveled and said to those who followed him, "Truly, I tell you, with no one in Israel have I found such faith."

– MATTHEW 8:8-10

The centurion was a leader who appreciated authority. He knew he had the full command of his subordinates, as they were subject to him. But he also acknowledged that there were some who outranked him. So when Jesus arrived on the scene, the centurion immediately confessed his place and gave respect to the authority of Jesus. Even Jesus expressed surprise at his approach.

But it was the faith, not only the leadership posture of the centurion, that caused Jesus to marvel. A glance into this moment in history reveals an affirmation of the soldier's humility, an example for Jesus' people to follow, and an encouragement to you today. Jesus celebrates the person of faith who submits to his authority.

Prayer

GOD, I do not often enough trust your authority in my life. Every situation and circumstance of my day falls under your control and domain. Today, rather than boast in the victories of the day or protest the challenges, I recognize they all come from you. I humbly submit to you today.

REFLECTION & DISCUSSION

ADMIT: What feelings does this topic invoke?

BRING: What issues do you need to address?

INFORM: What does the text say to do?

DETERMINE: What steps do you need to take?

EXECUTE: What action will you take?

SEEING

When they arrived, Samuel saw Eliab and thought, "Surely the Lord's anointed stands here before the Lord." But the Lord said to Samuel, "Do not consider his appearance or his height, for I have rejected him. The Lord does not look at the things people look at. People look at the outward appearance, but the Lord looks at the heart."

– 1 SAMUEL 16:6-7

We see the world differently than God. When God led Samuel to anoint the next king, Samuel laid eyes on eight distinct men, but he failed to see them as God did. By outward appearance, Eliab was a natural choice. He was tall and looked the part of a king, yet God wasn't concerned with those attributes. In a mentoring moment, God encouraged Samuel to take a second look. As God explained to Samuel, a leader fit to be a king and leader of God's people is qualified by his heart, not his appearance.

Recall this interchange whenever you are tempted to assess someone by their appearance and remember that a woman's heart is of first importance to God. We live in a world that celebrates physical attractiveness and human accomplishments, passing judgment on any who fail to measure up - and totally disregarding the qualities of a person's heart. Don't fall into that trap. Look around and pray that you will see others from God's perspective.

Prayer

GOD, I want you to help me see everyone I encounter today with spiritual eyes. Help me understand their heart and not get distracted by outward appearances.

REFLECTION & DISCUSSION

ADMIT: What feelings does this topic invoke?

BRING: What issues do you need to address?

INFORM: What does the text say to do?

DETERMINE: What steps do you need to take?

EXECUTE: What action will you take?

WORSHIP

"I appeal to you therefore, brothers, by the mercies of God, to present your bodies as a living sacrifice, holy and acceptable to God, which is your spiritual worship."

– ROMANS 12:1

$\mathcal{W}$orship is different than you think it is. It's not a musical presentation by a band, an event you attend weekly with a crowd of people, or entertainment that stirs you emotionally. Instead, it's a willing presentation of your being and all its facilities completely and continually to God.

In addition, it's done from a motivation of mercy across many moments. As you navigate your day, refuse to withhold your mercy or reduce worship to a moment. What you are doing right now is not a single disconnected moment of devotion and worship; it's a life of continual devotion and worship. Refuse to silo your thoughts, behaviors, and motivations because God wants you to give your all to Him - that's everything.

Prayer

GOD, today I want to worship you more fully than I did yesterday. And I desire to do this not to earn your approval but because I want to be a vessel for your mercy to others. Help me to keep you front of mind all day today. And when this fades from my awareness, bring it back to my worshipful attention.

REFLECTION & DISCUSSION

ADMIT: What feelings does this topic invoke?

BRING: What issues do you need to address?

INFORM: What does the text say to do?

DETERMINE: What steps do you need to take?

EXECUTE: What action will you take?

OUTRAGEOUS

"Have faith in God," Jesus answered. "Truly I tell you, if anyone says to this mountain, 'Go, throw yourself into the sea,' and does not doubt in their heart but believes that what they say will happen, it will be done for them. Therefore I tell you, whatever you ask for in prayer, believe that you have received it, and it will be yours."

– MARK 11:22-24

*M*ost of us never experience outrageous things because we never dream of outrageous things. We are scared to hope or pray outrageous things because it feels unrealistic. Here, Jesus dares you to believe, act, and pray beyond all sensible limits. He invites you to engage in a tremendous adventure beyond what reasonable people would think possible. Really, a mountain being thrown into the sea?

But the essential point is true: God's power is limitless. Unfortunately, our faith tends to struggle to catch up. Whenever you notice your faith shrinking, when you find yourself lowering your expectations of what God can do around and through you, remember Jesus' incredible invitation. Then boldly ask. Believe. Anticipate. And see what incredible, impossible, outrageous acts of God will follow.

Prayer

GOD, I have limited you in my life with weak prayers and small faith. My petty requests have only reinforced small thinking and have belittled the great things you want to do for and through me. God, today I bring big and outrageous prayers to you, believing you will do great things as my great God.

REFLECTION & DISCUSSION

ADMIT: What feelings does this topic invoke?

BRING: What issues do you need to address?

INFORM: What does the text say to do?

DETERMINE: What steps do you need to take?

EXECUTE: What action will you take?

VALUABLE

On the contrary, we speak as those approved by God to be entrusted with the gospel.

– 1 THESSALONIANS 2:4

*H*ave you ever been given something of great value? Maybe an heirloom, an antique, or an estate has been passed down to you. When someone entrusts you with something of value, you're naturally going to protect and preserve it at all costs. And is not the saving message of Jesus Christ the most precious gift given? We protect this message not by concealing it, but by freely sharing it with others.

The eternal fate of every individual hinges on the good news taught to us by Jesus Christ. This Word was revealed to us in, by, and through him. We guard it by allowing it to prove and shape us, and then generously sharing its lessons with others who, in turn, do the same. Reflect today on the value of the Word of God by considering the lessons it has taught you over time - the lessons that have shaped your life. And then multiply their value by sharing them with another friend, neighbor, or family member.

Prayer

GOD, today I am committing to share with others the lessons from your Word that have shaped my life. Help me to recall the stories and teachings and convey the truths within them so that people will see you and the freedom you provide. Thanks for entrusting me with this opportunity.

REFLECTION & DISCUSSION

ADMIT: What feelings does this topic invoke?

BRING: What issues do you need to address?

INFORM: What does the text say to do?

DETERMINE: What steps do you need to take?

EXECUTE: What action will you take?

BREATHE

All Scripture is breathed out by God and profitable for teaching, for reproof, for correction, and for training in righteousness, that the man of God may be complete, equipped for every good work.
– 2 TIMOTHY 3:16-17

*F*or a moment, take a deep breath - one deep breath in and out. Deep breathing techniques have been used for years to reduce stress and anxiety. On an even more fundamental level, the very act of breathing keeps you alive - and the same is true in the spiritual life. Breath from God is what first activated life in humankind, and the breath of God's Word is what activates spiritual life in us today. Do you want to be successful? Are you interested in being complete? Then take a spiritual breath.

Woman of God, take God's Word and breathe it in. Meditate on it until your spiritual breathing becomes as unconscious as the breath you just took. For a woman disciplined in spiritual breathing is a righteous woman equipped to succeed and act in every good work.

Prayer

GOD, I want to develop an unconscious pattern of breathing. Help me take steps to address the issues that inhibit me; give me joy and fulfillment every time I dig into your Word.

REFLECTION & DISCUSSION

ADMIT: What feelings does this topic invoke?

BRING: What issues do you need to address?

INFORM: What does the text say to do?

DETERMINE: What steps do you need to take?

EXECUTE: What action will you take?

TRUSTED

Trust in the Lord with all your heart and lean not on your own understanding; in all your ways submit to him, and he will make your paths straight.

– PROVERBS 3:5-6

The definition of trust is an unshakable belief in the ability, truth, reliability, or strength of a person or an object. When it comes to everyday trust, there are brands you use because, over time, you have found them trustworthy. The more experience you have with a product or process, the more trust you have in its performance. In the same way, trusting relationships take time to build; there is no shortcut.

Building trust with God requires entering a relationship with him. To experience the trustworthiness of his Person, you must demonstrate vulnerability and take a risk, and the risk you take is called faith. By faith, entrust your life to God and invite him to prove his character. Give yourself entirely to him and test his unwavering integrity and truth that will never let you down.

Prayer

GOD, I put my faith in many things, but nothing is as promising and sure as placing my faith in you. Grow my trust by helping me take leaps of faith, and in return, be faithful to me one day at a time, giving me a path through every circumstance.

REFLECTION & DISCUSSION

ADMIT: What feelings does this topic invoke?

BRING: What issues do you need to address?

INFORM: What does the text say to do?

DETERMINE: What steps do you need to take?

EXECUTE: What action will you take?

QUALIFIED

Now when they saw the boldness of Peter and John and perceived that they were uneducated, common men, they were astonished. And they recognized that they had been with Jesus. But seeing the man who was healed standing beside them, they had nothing to say in opposition.

– ACTS 4:13-14

*A*fter a miraculous healing and an inspired presentation of the gospel message, the onlookers were in shock. The religious leaders could not understand what they had just seen. Peter and John were a human contradiction: unusually bold and articulate, yet devoid of formal training and education. What made them *"uncommon?"* They had spent time with Jesus.

We all have days when we feel unqualified. It is a feeling that leads to apathy. When those feelings rise up in you, remember that Peter and John boldly spoke and acted with power, and their only qualification was the time they spent with Jesus. Jesus said it this way: *"Remain in me, as I also remain in you. No branch can bear fruit by itself; it must remain in the vine. Neither can you bear fruit unless you remain in me"* (John 15:4). That's it, nothing more - time with the Master qualifies you to act boldly on his behalf.

Prayer

GOD, I run into most days giving little time and attention to you. Usually, this leads to exhaustion and a feeling of emptiness. Fill me today with strength and let the time I invest with you give me a boldness that shocks the world.

REFLECTION & DISCUSSION

ADMIT: What feelings does this topic invoke?

BRING: What issues do you need to address?

INFORM: What does the text say to do?

DETERMINE: What steps do you need to take?

EXECUTE: What action will you take?

PURPOSED

For by grace you have been saved through faith. And this is not your own doing; it is the gift of God, not a result of works, so that no one may boast. For we are his workmanship, created in Christ Jesus for good works, which God prepared beforehand, that we should walk in them.

– EPHESIANS 2:8-10

There is nothing more motivating than purpose. Consider for a moment a time when you felt no or little purpose in a task you had to accomplish. A lack of purpose can have devastating consequences and lead one to self-destruct. On the other hand, a clear sense of purpose inspires women toward a satisfying future.

You did not enter this world purposeless! And your role here is not to create your purpose; it is to discover it. God, the Creator, creates with a purpose. He designed humanity purposefully. No craftsman develops something without a use in mind. You are God's workmanship. You are created for good works. God planned your meaningful involvement in his creation and has demonstrated over time that he chooses to work through you. And the one role you have is to live out that purpose; in all things glorify him. Take aim at the great purpose of God.

Prayer

GOD, thanks for designing me perfectly and beautifully. Bring attention to your glory through me in this day. May your purposes be seen in my life and my good works.

REFLECTION & DISCUSSION

ADMIT: What feelings does this topic invoke?

BRING: What issues do you need to address?

INFORM: What does the text say to do?

DETERMINE: What steps do you need to take?

EXECUTE: What action will you take?

FILLED

Make a tree good and its fruit will be good, or make a tree bad and its fruit will be bad, for a tree is recognized by its fruit. You brood of vipers, how can you who are evil say anything good? For the mouth speaks what the heart is full of. A good man brings good things out of the good stored up in him, and an evil man brings evil things out of the evil stored up in him.

– MATTHEW 12:33-35

When you accidentally knock over a glass, what happens? Liquid spills out. What sort of liquid? The kind you filled it with, of course. In the same way, Jesus taught that the heart is like a glass - a vessel. What comes out of your mouth reflects what lies within the vessel of your heart. For that reason, it is imperative to pay attention to what is being poured into and out of the vessel.

As God's vessel, you can't avoid the disruptions of life, but you can ensure your reaction will honor God. Out of the overflow of your heart, you will respond. Every woman is always spilling her life out before others. These *"spills"* are some of the most significant teachable moments because they happen so frequently, so spill out God's best today.

Prayer

GOD, I am not the best at regulating my mouth. But I see that maybe the issue is what I am putting in my heart. My heart is full of conflict, and I pray today you will fill me with grace and love so that my words and actions will reflect you.

REFLECTION & DISCUSSION

ADMIT: What feelings does this topic invoke?

BRING: What issues do you need to address?

INFORM: What does the text say to do?

DETERMINE: What steps do you need to take?

EXECUTE: What action will you take?

FREED

⸎

But whenever anyone turns to the Lord, the veil is taken away. Now the Lord is the Spirit, and where the Spirit of the Lord is, there is freedom.

– 2 CORINTHIANS 3:16-17

⸎

*B*y nature, humans long for freedom. We don't always know how to articulate this, but old patterns and perceptions keep us in prisons and from our true freedom. Some women want to be free to do something, while others want to be free from something. But real freedom is found only in Christ - in the Spirit of the Lord.

God knows what his creation, humankind, needs. There is no question that Jesus Christ's entrance into the world resolved the greatest need you have as a woman: freedom from sin and the ramifications of spiritual and physical death. Jesus' victory provides you with victory over both, through his life, death, and resurrection. Through him, you have freedom. He releases you from your old destructive habits and insecurities and calls you to new life in him.

Prayer

GOD, I don't deserve your freedom, but you generously gave it to me. Today, I give thanks to you for giving me your Son in whom I have freedom from all past sins, trading death for eternal life.

REFLECTION & DISCUSSION

ADMIT: What feelings does this topic invoke?

BRING: What issues do you need to address?

INFORM: What does the text say to do?

DETERMINE: What steps do you need to take?

EXECUTE: What action will you take?

CHANGED

But he said to me, "My grace is sufficient for you, for my power is made perfect in weakness." Therefore I will boast all the more gladly of my weaknesses, so that the power of Christ may rest upon me. For the sake of Christ, then, I am content with weaknesses, insults, hardships, persecutions, and calamities. For when I am weak, then I am strong.
– 2 CORINTHIANS 12:9-10

*L*ife produces countless moments that pit inner desires against each other. These moments are uncomfortable and will often send you to God in prayer, seeking relief. This was Paul's experience. He describes a *"thorn in his flesh"* that caused him frequent discomfort. He begged God to remove the thorn, but God said no and urged Paul to rethink his situation. Paul finally understood that every trial was an opportunity for God to prove his grace and power.

Sometimes what a woman thinks she needs and what she actually needs are two entirely different things. Paul felt he needed this thorn removed, yet God knew the thorn was necessary. So Paul allowed God's Word to change his thinking rather than change his situation. The next time you want relief from a painful moment, but don't get what you're asking for, invite God to change your thinking by grounding yourself in his Word. See more opportunities to boast in weakness and fewer reasons to complain. Be content by following Paul's example.

Prayer

GOD, I often want you to change my situation rather than change me. I confess I immediately ask for a way out. And while I know you can change any circumstance; it is often me that needs to change. Change my mind today about my issues!

45

REFLECTION & DISCUSSION

ADMIT: What feelings does this topic invoke?

BRING: What issues do you need to address?

INFORM: What does the text say to do?

DETERMINE: What steps do you need to take?

EXECUTE: What action will you take?

THANKFUL

Know that the Lord, he is God! It is he who made us, and we are his; we are his people, and the sheep of his pasture. Enter his gates with thanksgiving, and his courts with praise! Give thanks to him; bless his name! For the Lord is good; his steadfast love endures forever, and his faithfulness to all generations.

– PSALM 100:3-5

*T*hink about the last time you observed an act of ungratefulness. Seeing this can be difficult. Young children, for example, are often ungrateful, usually because they lack perspective and an understanding of the cost or sacrifice. On the other hand, the one who practices giving thanks has a significant impact on the giver and those who witness the exchange. When you read through Psalms, you see that David offers thanks during the good times and the bad. The practice of praising God causes the heart to receive a blessing no matter the circumstances.

God is good, steadfast, eternal, and faithful to all generations. He created us and concerns himself with our well-being. You are a recipient of his crazy generosity. Living a life of gratitude may start by saying *"thank you,"* but gratitude becomes entrenched in life when one realizes the extent of who God is and what he has done. When you take the time to evaluate your life and recognize even the smallest detail of God's faithfulness to you, thankfulness becomes habitual. Tune your heart to know the character of God by choosing to be thankful always.

Prayer

GOD, I don't say thanks enough, so I apologize for my ingratitude. Like a stubborn daughter, my heart overlooks all you have done in my life. Today, receive my thanks.

REFLECTION & DISCUSSION

ADMIT: What feelings does this topic invoke?

BRING: What issues do you need to address?

INFORM: What does the text say to do?

DETERMINE: What steps do you need to take?

EXECUTE: What action will you take?

GLORIFY

Jesus replied, "If I glorify myself, my glory means nothing. My Father, whom you claim as your God, is the one who glorifies me. Though you do not know him, I know him. If I said I did not, I would be a liar like you, but I do know him and obey his word."
– JOHN 8:54-55

We live in a world that promotes self. Social media becomes a stage upon which we celebrate our own success. There are many other ways women seek glory, but glory-seeking is not the activity of a follower of God. Jesus had no interest in glorifying himself. He had every opportunity to do so and was even tempted by Satan in this same way, but he stayed focused on deflecting glory to God. His thoughts and actions were in close alignment on this matter. Knowing that self-glorification was a meaningless activity, Jesus glorified his Father.

As followers, we emulate the thoughts and actions of Jesus. This posture is not self-inflating or self-glorifying. Instead, it's an entirely humble posture that seeks to *"acknowledge that Jesus Christ is Lord, to the glory of God the Father"* (Philippians 2:11). The object of any glory should be God himself. Rest assured you will have to make a decision to either chase fame or redirect all glory to the One who deserves it all.

Prayer

GOD, I give you glory today for what you have done in me and through me. May I never be a glory-stealer; please prompt and remind me to deflect to you.

REFLECTION & DISCUSSION

ADMIT: What feelings does this topic invoke?

BRING: What issues do you need to address?

INFORM: What does the text say to do?

DETERMINE: What steps do you need to take?

EXECUTE: What action will you take?

TESTIFY

For I delivered to you as of first importance what I also received: that Christ died for our sins in accordance with the Scriptures, that he was buried, that he was raised on the third day in accordance with the Scriptures, and that he appeared to Cephas, then to the twelve. Then he appeared to more than five hundred brothers at one time, most of whom are still alive, though some have fallen asleep. Then he appeared to James, then to all the apostles. Last of all, as to one untimely born, he appeared also to me.

– 1 CORINTHIANS 13:3-8

*A*n eyewitness is one who testifies to what they perceived through their senses. Over 500 individuals could testify to the validity of the disciples' claim that Christ rose from the dead. Among these witnesses was a person who wrote nearly half of the New Testament books - Paul the apostle.

Paul thought it was critically important to pass along the truth of Christ's death, burial, and resurrection. His priority was to deliver his testimony concerning Jesus Christ. How can you follow Paul's example? By appropriately prioritizing what you testify about. Your life tells a story through the way you interact with the world around you. As a follower of Christ, emulating Paul's passion for the gospel is an example worth following.

Prayer

GOD, give me strength today to share my story with one other person – even just a clip from my life. I pray you will provide me with both courage and opportunity.

REFLECTION & DISCUSSION

ADMIT: What feelings does this topic invoke?

BRING: What issues do you need to address?

INFORM: What does the text say to do?

DETERMINE: What steps do you need to take?

EXECUTE: What action will you take?

SACRIFICE

I am the good shepherd. The good shepherd lays down his life for the sheep. The hired hand is not the shepherd and does not own the sheep. So when he sees the wolf coming, he abandons the sheep and runs away. Then the wolf attacks the flock and scatters it. The man runs away because he is a hired hand and cares nothing for the sheep. I am the good shepherd; I know my sheep and my sheep know me – just as the Father knows me and I know the Father – and I lay down my life for the sheep. I have other sheep that are not of this sheep pen. I must bring them also. They too will listen to my voice, and there shall be one flock and one shepherd.

– JOHN 10:11-16

The difference between the good shepherd and the hired hand is ownership. The action of the shepherd is selfless and personal, demonstrating both courage and commitment. The hired hand is wavering, concerned with self-preservation, and has no concern for the sheep. As Jesus shared this lesson, his cross was surely on his mind. Consider for a moment how much more meaningful this story must have been to the disciples after they, his sheep, witnessed their Master, the Shepherd, laying down his life for them as he promised he would!

At the moment of necessary sacrifice, the opportunity for leadership reveals itself. Trials expose the depth of your concern for others, showing exactly how much you are willing to sacrifice to safeguard their well-being. When Jesus laid his life down, he set the standard for sacrifice. We now have a perfect example of a leader whom we are called to emulate. Paul was correct when he said, *"In your relationships with one another, have the same mindset as Christ Jesus."* Self-sacrifice out of love for the Father must decorate the landscape of our relationships.

Prayer

GOD, help me to be sacrificial. May I model my life after your sacrificial way, not for my benefit but so that others will see you.

REFLECTION & DISCUSSION

ADMIT: What feelings does this topic invoke?

BRING: What issues do you need to address?

INFORM: What does the text say to do?

DETERMINE: What steps do you need to take?

EXECUTE: What action will you take?

SHARE

⧫

But if I say, "I will not mention his word or speak any more in his name," his word is in my heart like a fire, a fire shut up in my bones. I am weary of holding it in; indeed, I cannot.

– JEREMIAH 20:9

⧫

*Y*ou can hear the deep conflict in the words of the prophet Jeremiah. He was the bearer of horrifying news, chosen by God to deliver an unpopular message. But the Word of God is a dominant force inside of a woman. When God places his instruction on your heart, the urge to act is almost irresistible.

How exciting is it that we have been given the good news! His Word to us in this day and age is a wonderful one to deliver to humanity. Does this message of hope in Jesus cause the same fire to burn in your heart? Today would be a great day to thank God, as we have the privilege of delivering this message. Ask God to light that fire within you, to compel you to share his Word to the point of weariness if you dare to hold it in.

Prayer

GOD, may your words burn within my heart. Give me a heart overflowing with your compassion and an irresistible call like you gave to Jeremiah. May I not hold back from sharing your good news to the world.

REFLECTION & DISCUSSION

ADMIT: What feelings does this topic invoke?

BRING: What issues do you need to address?

INFORM: What does the text say to do?

DETERMINE: What steps do you need to take?

EXECUTE: What action will you take?

FOLLOW

"Fellow Israelites, listen to this: Jesus of Nazareth was a man accredited by God to you by miracles, wonders and signs, which God did among you through him, as you yourselves know. This man was handed over to you by God's deliberate plan and foreknowledge; and you, with the help of wicked men, put him to death by nailing him to the cross. But God raised him from the dead, freeing him from the agony of death, because it was impossible for death to keep its hold on him... Therefore let all Israel be assured of this: God has made this Jesus, whom you crucified, both Lord and Messiah."

– ACTS 2:22-24, 36

*T*he first people who witnessed the life of Christ and his resurrection understood this event the best. Peter and the other disciples had a first-hand look at everything that unfolded. Their firsthand testimony should always be at the forefront of our minds, as they were expert witnesses. Pay close attention to Peter's emphasis. His primary concern was to establish that Jesus was God's Son evidenced by signs, which they too had seen. As people in the crowd began to believe this message, Peter then told them the best way to respond: to repent and be baptized. In other words, they needed to pledge loyalty to Christ and follow him.

The death and resurrection of Christ give way to a natural process of self-evaluation as a woman and a servant of Christ. Invite God to reveal areas where you might reject his leadership and pray for the courage to let him direct you. Remember that Jesus modeled this lifestyle of reflection and submission as a leader who acted on the Father's will, even as it led him down a challenging path to the cross. Identify the situations in your life where you try to exert your will instead of allowing God to lead. Then offer God your full-hearted obedience.

Prayer

GOD, I know there are areas where I have not given you lordship in my life. Reveal these areas and help me surrender to your leadership.

REFLECTION & DISCUSSION

ADMIT: What feelings does this topic invoke?

BRING: What issues do you need to address?

INFORM: What does the text say to do?

DETERMINE: What steps do you need to take?

EXECUTE: What action will you take?

SHINE

And Jesus cried out and said, "Whoever believes in me, believes not in me but in him who sent me. And whoever sees me sees him who sent me. I have come into the world as light, so that whoever believes in me may not remain in darkness. If anyone hears my words and does not keep them, I do not judge him; for I did not come to judge the world but to save the world. The one who rejects me and does not receive my words has a judge; the word that I have spoken will judge him on the last day."

– JOHN 12:44-48

*J*esus was the perfect example of someone who understood God's mission. So Jesus was faithful to reveal God and his plan of salvation. Through Jesus' obedience, light came into the world so that darkness and all its effects would not prevail. Belief in Jesus brings salvation, and with it light that gives spiritual sight. Darkness causes chaos and poor decisions leading to spiritual blindness, but the clarity of the light brings freedom.

Everyone grapples with seeing clearly. Questions about who you are and what you are meant to do swirl in your mind at your most honest and sobering moments. But Jesus paints a picture of a focused and determined follower. As you prepare to lead those around you, be focused like Christ in revealing the truth. Shed light on Christ by purposefully demonstrating his love to all those around you and be prepared to explain the hope you have in Christ.

Prayer

GOD, I am not always in the light, but today I commit to reflect the light of Christ. May my life reflect all your glory in this often-dark world.

REFLECTION & DISCUSSION

ADMIT: What feelings does this topic invoke?

BRING: What issues do you need to address?

INFORM: What does the text say to do?

DETERMINE: What steps do you need to take?

EXECUTE: What action will you take?

LEAD

Wives, submit to your husbands, as is fitting in the Lord. Husbands, love your wives and do not be harsh with them.

– COLOSSIANS 3:18-19

Naturally, there is a great deal of debate among Christians about what these words mean, especially given the changes in culture since they were written. Some husbands wonder, *"What does it look like to live this out?"* And some wives ask, *"Why does he get to be the spiritual leader? Can't we both do it?"* In the end, it all comes down to how we define leadership.

A biblically sound definition of spiritual leadership doesn't imply that the person being led is inferior, inadequate, or of less importance. And a biblical interpretation does not preclude those being led from leading others, using their gifts, and contributing to decisions. For an excellent definition of leadership, we only need to look to the life of Jesus Christ, the most celebrated spiritual leader of all time. He did not force the power and position of his role on others but used his power and position to serve others in this world – and in the end, he himself submitted to his Father. Consider Jesus' example as you live out your role as a wife, mother, and leader.

Prayer

GOD, help me navigate the maze of leadership but, more importantly, help me be the right person in all roles of my life. God, nudge me to serve and love others today.

REFLECTION & DISCUSSION

ADMIT: What feelings does this topic invoke?

BRING: What issues do you need to address?

INFORM: What does the text say to do?

DETERMINE: What steps do you need to take?

EXECUTE: What action will you take?

TREASURE

Do not lay up for yourselves treasures on earth, where moth and rust destroy and where thieves break in and steal, but lay up for yourselves treasures in heaven, where neither moth nor rust destroys and where thieves do not break in and steal. For where your treasure is, there your heart will be also. The eye is the lamp of the body. So, if your eye is healthy, your whole body will be full of light, but if your eye is bad, your whole body will be full of darkness. If then the light in you is darkness, how great is the darkness! No one can serve two masters, for either he will hate the one and love the other, or he will be devoted to the one and despise the other. You cannot serve God and money.

– MATTHEW 6:19-24

*P*eople love to pursue things that trigger self-advancement. There is a sense of urgency when motivation is at its peak. Jesus knows our hearts and gives clear direction around one big motivator - treasures of this earth. The allure of treasure has the power to drag your heart - and by extension your whole person - into or out of a relationship with God. It can alter your motivations and determine your spiritual trajectory.

But treasures can be found both on earth and in heaven. Treasure of any kind isn't morally good or bad - it can be a gift of God's provision, the spoils of moral corruption, or simply wages earned. But no matter its source, treasure is extremely powerful, able to affect your emotions, morality, and behaviors. Guard your heart from greed, jealousy, and anxiety, thanking God for his provision. Then savor the priceless, eternal gift you have in Christ.

Prayer

GOD, earthly treasures consume me. I store these up to no avail. I do this because my possessions make me feel secure and powerful. God, hear my confession and help me to hold the treasures of this world loosely.

REFLECTION & DISCUSSION

ADMIT: What feelings does this topic invoke?

BRING: What issues do you need to address?

INFORM: What does the text say to do?

DETERMINE: What steps do you need to take?

EXECUTE: What action will you take?

FORWARD

But, dear friends, remember what the apostles of our Lord Jesus Christ foretold. They said to you, "In the last times there will be scoffers who will follow their own ungodly desires." These are the people who divide you, who follow mere natural instincts and do not have the Spirit. But you, dear friends, by building yourselves up in your most holy faith and praying in the Holy Spirit, keep yourselves in God's love as you wait for the mercy of our Lord Jesus Christ to bring you to eternal life. Be merciful to those who doubt; save others by snatching them from the fire; to others show mercy, mixed with fear – hating even the clothing stained by corrupted flesh.
– JUDE 17-23

Jude wrote a short book with a powerful message. In twenty-four verses, he gives us a wise outlook on how to persevere and move forward in the faith. He points out the current circumstances and contrasts two types of people: those who follow their natural instincts and those who are led by the Spirit. If you follow the Spirit, you will be building on your faith with prayer. With eternal life in view, you wait within the love of Christ. You are merciful toward others and despise sin.

A distinct picture of what it means to be a woman in Christ comes into focus when you daily move forward with God. *"Following ungodly desires,"* on the other hand, distracts you from this following. Should you find yourself in this moment, the remedy is trust in the Holy Spirit in lieu of God's mercy, which is soon to come. Remember, our enemy is constantly trying to separate you from community, devotion, and basic biblical practices. He wants to keep you from moving forward. Remind yourself to stay on mission and strive to move forward, following God's lead.

Prayer

GOD, you are always the source of my strength. Bring to my attention my ungodly desires and foster in me a new heart and spirit that desire you.

REFLECTION & DISCUSSION

ADMIT: What feelings does this topic invoke?

BRING: What issues do you need to address?

INFORM: What does the text say to do?

DETERMINE: What steps do you need to take?

EXECUTE: What action will you take?

POINT

From Miletus, Paul sent to Ephesus for the elders of the church. When they arrived, he said to them: "You know how I lived the whole time I was with you, from the first day I came into the province of Asia. I served the Lord with great humility and with tears and in the midst of severe testing by the plots of my Jewish opponents. You know that I have not hesitated to preach anything that would be helpful to you but have taught you publicly and from house to house. I have declared to both Jews and Greeks that they must turn to God in repentance and have faith in our Lord Jesus."

– ACTS 20:17-21

*P*aul knew that his time was short and that his mission was nearly complete. His ministry career had been impactful and far-reaching. Not only did God use him to spread the gospel during his time on earth, but even today, we read these words and receive wisdom and insight from this apostle. As Paul traveled toward Jerusalem, he made a point to speak one last time to the church leaders in Ephesus. He reminded them of the trials they had endured together and urged them strongly to keep the faith.

Paul referenced his own life as a testimony to Jesus. He had shown generosity and resolve in sharing Christ with them, even in the midst of persecution. He never hesitated to teach the gospel, and he taught with complete transparency. You should ask yourself if your life is evidence of the message you share verbally. Can you leverage your experiences as Paul did with his? Be encouraged that Paul recovered from many missteps early on. Challenge yourself to serve the Lord today so at the end of your life, like Paul, you can boldly declare, *"You know how I lived..."*

Prayer

GOD, help me point to you both in what I do and what I say. May my life be the best example possible as I live in your strength.

REFLECTION & DISCUSSION

ADMIT: What feelings does this topic invoke?

BRING: What issues do you need to address?

INFORM: What does the text say to do?

DETERMINE: What steps do you need to take?

EXECUTE: What action will you take?

MENTOR

Now the eleven disciples went to Galilee, to the mountain to which Jesus had directed them. And when they saw him they worshiped him, but some doubted. And Jesus came and said to them, "All authority in heaven and on earth has been given to me. Go therefore and make disciples of all nations, baptizing them in the name of the Father and of the Son and of the Holy Spirit, teaching them to observe all that I have commanded you. And behold, I am with you always, to the end of the age."

– MATTHEW 28:16-20

Throughout Scripture, mountains were a special place where God often revealed his Word. He delivered the Ten Commandments to his people on a mount, and from a mount, Jesus commissioned his people. He gave them one thing to do: make more disciples. The process of discipleship was the only method offered for preserving the church, and Jesus continues to hang the hopes of the world on the success of his followers. The command Jesus gave at the end of his life on earth applies to us today. All who follow Jesus are responsible to find and equip new followers.

God has involved us in his discipleship plans from the very beginning of time. A follower who shares Christ and trains others in the faith has modeled his activities after what Jesus did. Jesus spent time with his disciples and led them to think and act as God's ambassadors. Take some time today to think about women you can disciple and mentor. Be intentionally obedient to Jesus by going forth and engaging others.

Prayer

GOD, the call to discipleship is overwhelming to me, but I must be obedient. Give me someone to disciple and mentor; put him in my path today.

REFLECTION & DISCUSSION

ADMIT: What feelings does this topic invoke?

BRING: What issues do you need to address?

INFORM: What does the text say to do?

DETERMINE: What steps do you need to take?

EXECUTE: What action will you take?

COMMUNICATE

✿

So Moses thought, "I will go over and see this strange sight – why the bush does not burn up."

And now the cry of the Israelites has reached me, and I have seen the way the Egyptians are oppressing them. So now, go. I am sending you to Pharaoh to bring my people the Israelites out of Egypt." But Moses said to God, "Who am I that I should go to Pharaoh and bring the Israelites out of Egypt?" And God said, "I will be with you. And this will be the sign to you that it is I who have sent you: When you have brought the people out of Egypt, you will worship God on this mountain.

– EXODUS 3:3, 9-12

✿

*G*od lured Moses in with a strange sight - a burning bush. A dry bush in an arid region should not take long to burn completely, so the miracle became more apparent the longer Moses watched. Once he was totally transfixed, God spoke. While the bush was an unusual sight, it was not to be worshipped or regarded as powerful itself. Through God, any tool he purposes will be productive.

Just as an ordinary bush became something extraordinary when God inhabited it, God would make Moses into an irresistible ambassador for his people. Moses was nothing without God, but equipped with God's powerful presence, victory became a foregone conclusion. God is with you also and calls you to join in the mission. *"Go make disciples"* was the last instruction Jesus gave his church, and you can be confident that God will be with you as you obey.

Prayer

GOD, you design moments and opportunities. Today, let me experience something unique. Provide a moment to converse about you with someone else. And I pray that the person I speak with will see you.

REFLECTION & DISCUSSION

ADMIT: What feelings does this topic invoke?

BRING: What issues do you need to address?

INFORM: What does the text say to do?

DETERMINE: What steps do you need to take?

EXECUTE: What action will you take?

EAGER

And the Spirit said to Philip, "Go over and join this chariot." So Philip ran to him and heard him reading Isaiah the prophet and asked, "Do you understand what you are reading?" And he said, "How can I, unless someone guides me?" And he invited Philip to come up and sit with him. And the eunuch said to Philip, "...About whom, I ask you, does the prophet say this, about himself or about someone else?" Then Philip opened his mouth, and beginning with this Scripture he told him the good news about Jesus.

– ACTS 8:29-31, 34-35

*P*hilip was an eager follower who ran in the direction given to him. When the Spirit gave instruction, there was no hesitation. The approach Philip took was rather simplistic. He listened, assessed the situation, asked a question, and responded. All it took for this life-transforming conversation to unfold was Philip's obedience while the Spirit provided all the leadership. This dialogue resulted in the advancement of the gospel in the heart of one seeking direction.

We often are quick to disqualify ourselves when it comes to sharing the gospel with others. Excuses range from *"I don't want to be holier-than- thou"* to *"I don't know what to say."* Notice that anyone can implement the pattern laid out by Philip. It only requires a willing heart. Be eager to listen to the Spirit's leadership and to those around you and respond by sharing the good news.

Prayer

GOD, while I may not be Philip, I am called by you and that is enough for me. I tend to question my ability, but I need to stop disqualifying myself. Empower me with the Holy Spirit to be courageous and share you with others.

REFLECTION & DISCUSSION

ADMIT: What feelings does this topic invoke?

BRING: What issues do you need to address?

INFORM: What does the text say to do?

DETERMINE: What steps do you need to take?

EXECUTE: What action will you take?